S0-FNS-559

Copyright © 2003 Nathaniel Brunson

ISBN: 1-59196-239-0

For information and to purchase additional copies:
www.diggidypoet.com

All rights reserved.
No part of this book may be reproduced, stored in retrieval systems or transmitted in any form, by any means, including mechanical, electronic, recording, photocopying, or otherwise without the express written permission of the author and publisher. For information on permission for reprints or excerpts please contact the publisher.

The title is a registered trademark and copyright of the author.

PoeticJava Publishing is a trademark of the publisher and the cup is a registered trademark of www.muggajava.com.
All rights reserved.

This book is also available in eBook format.

PoeticJava Publishing
www.write4us.com
creativitywanted@write4us.com

Hollering At My Peeps

Even though I am very closed off, aloof, and stubborn at times, I do have to thank those whom impacted and affected my life the most, bringing me to be where I am today.

My mom, with all of her guidance and encouragement, believing in me when I didn't even believe in myself, giving me the name Nathaniel meaning a gift of God, making me believe that I am what my name states I am a true "gift of God". I love you so much ma, and don't know what I'd do without you.

My sisters Sherry, and Lynnette- for teaching me how to stand up for myself, and for holding me to such high standards, which even though at times I could not maintain them, it gave me the drive to be all that I can possibly be.

To my dad- for allowing me the freedom to choose my own path.

My little sisters Anntoinette, and Victoria, my little brother Vincent, and my nieces Tieara and Teyonna.

To Roz– for supporting me and encouraging me to by my best even at my worst.

To my one and only B-Man– what can I say, you have been my muse, my inspiration, and my motivation to continue on, I'll love you to my death. Without you half of this book would not be! Our friendship allowed me to understand how to cope with the reality that sometimes love is a serious emotion that can be a beautiful thing on one's behalf, but never surface on another's. Through all of the ups and downs we've experienced I have grown to be who I am. Because of you I can honestly say that I am better man. Tell Lil-Jay that I miss him…

To my many friends who have been there through thick and thin, putting up with my temperament, and just taking the time to understand why I can be so self-reflective (centered) at times.

Jade- scruffy much love, My lil-sis Whitney you are gonna be the first woman President, Mama Anderson- for being a maternal figure in my life when I couldn't have my own mother.

To Jermaine- for keeping me on my toes and being so loving. I've learned so much from and by you. Good luck on your endeavors, you best believe that I am will always have your back. Tony- through our ups and downs you've always made me feel like I am the best.

Rebecca- for being such a major inspiration to my writings, you honestly are the one that made me step up my pen game, I can't wait until I am reading one of these from you (In The Minds of a Poet, forever).

Lekethia- you understand and compliment me so well. (I swear we were separated at birth) Thanks for being there.

To my peeps Deya, Alex, Crystal, Daavide, Tiffany Evans, Carolyn, Kelly Throne, Kendra, Ronika, and Christine.

To Ms. Hurt, and Ms Boyd my high school mentors, you guys helped me so much.

To the S&H Racecraft crew- Terry, Rob, Sue, and to anybody else who have supported me through the years who I may have forgotten.

Last but not least I would have to credit my God, for allowing me the ability to experience each day as it comes, whether I chose to embrace that day, or run away from it seems as though he's always kept me even when I didn't want to be kept. This has truly been a humbling experience, and without my God given talents, it wouldn't be possible.

Thanks everyone, hopefully you will enjoy, and maybe the traces of my emotions will enlighten your understanding of "Nate Diggidy."

To Ms. Vega:

Thanks for supporting me in my endeavors. I hope you enjoy "Tenses of my Emotion"

Peace and Blessings

Nate Dagody

Traces of My Emotion

-Nathaniel Brunson

Pt. One: In The Inside Looking Out

1. Manifest Destiny
2. It's Trite, so What's New?
3. The Life I Knew
4. Kiss of Death
5. Happiness isn't here
6. Nowhere to Hide
7. Forever Young
8. Senses of Imperfection
9. Time and Time Again
10. Love of my Life
11. Boiled Skin
12. The Ex-Factor (Factor Me Gone)
13. Continued
14. Untouchable Love
15. Back at One
16. Father to Son
17. Son to Father
18. Broken Chains
19. A Little Patience a lot of Progress
20. Burn the Bitch Down
21. Will This Get Trough to You
22. My Mind is Playing Tricks on Me
23. The Best of Me
24. Five Step Creep
25. Mommy Dearest
26. All That I Have
27. Hope for the Future
28. Opening Closed Doors
29. What it is...
30. Does anyone care?

Pt. Two: Spoken Silence

31. Open Mic
32. Fear Factor
33. Breathing in Silence
34. Married with Children
35. Once Again
36. Kiss of a Rose
37. Bottomless Pit
38. Hoping for the Best
39. The Limelight is Glowing Dim
40. Home Sweet Home
41. The Vibe
42. The Vibe Part II
43. The God in Me
44. Winter Storms of a Nightmare
45. Continued
46. More Than a Man
47. Continued
48. Reaching for the Untouched
49. The Writing is on the Walls
50. Feeling You
51. Jagged Little Pill
52. Smiles
53. Brotha Man
54. Flight 707
55. Kodak Moment
56. The Road less Traveled
57. The Best of Me Part II (A Year Later)
58. No one Cared (Does Anyone Care?)
59. Piecing it together Somehow
60. So you asked
61. Spring Flowers Every Hour
62. The Bastard Child in Me

Part I.

In The Inside Looking Out

Manifest Destiny

To flow this way oh no, how so but you watch,
Me now not vulgar, but still speak too profound
For you to evaluate, contemplate.
Heaven forsake I debut this for those to dispute.
With the placated, sedated, rhymes,
And Rhythms of previous escapisms.

Too hot to handle, like fire under the mantel.
Departing to be anomaly for me personally.
Footprints in the dust, I dictate syntax take note you must...
Of the lyricist, troubadour with a pen, you don't comprehend,
You can't take in, so don't even begin to pretend,
That you could flow superfluous to this.

To play my game you'd go insane,
Not knowing the tears to form metaphorically rain.
While my future gaped wide even with no one by my side...
Productions and reproductions of my brainchild that's how.
Your answer to the urge that inspires this in me.
Eccentric ness, eclecticism all in the past generating my manifest destiny.

It's Trite, so What's New?

Decades and centuries wasted.
Plaguing bitterness in our heads.
A complementary race, so looong the feeling.
That they make us grow to dread.

We weren't there though they do not realize.
We weren't living those slave years.
However, they instill in us contempt.
Forcing us to cry because of their tears.

So I ask myself why?
Why must we carry on the same old cliché?
Why must we act impiously?
Still blaming racism to this day.

Because honestly, inside of their heads,
They could give a damn about me.
Yet they want to me to live my life in their past.
So that I can empathize their misery.

Bearing an unwarranted theory.
That my superior is all thee that is white.
My superior is my God, myself,
The one whom I lie asleep with through the night.

Lingering on what is now superficial.
Like the existence of slave days.
As is my life isn't confusing enough.
Being an introverted maze.

Do they actually think that I care?
My ancestors were people I never knew.
Does the sun stop shinning,
Because centuries ago the moon glared blue?

It's redundant far too long now.
I can't stop my munificence because of history.
I have to make my own history,
That is what I know is life for this, for us, for me

The Life I Knew

Growing up as an individual.
For many years building stones, and leaving behind signature moments.
Embarking from authoritative concepts, and now I AM THREW.
I had to live life that way; it was the only life I knew.

Running to accomplish a future.
Striding for victory, crossing the line to capture my joy, my goals.
Running old, running so long that now I AM THREW.
I ran for fans, so I ran, and it was the only life I knew.

Living to make you guys happy.
Building a mystery, leaving me in mystery, and now I must gather
To find myself since you have left me behind when YOU WERE THREW…
With me because I lived against you…I lived the only life I knew.

Hiding my feelings behind.
Terrified that others would label me gay.
Pretending to my emotions, defending them from the pain of going through.
I've opened the doors, obscured no more, yet it was the life I knew.

Holding on to a cherished love.
A love untouched by no other, a love never touched by me.
Grasping for air, somewhere hoping that the cloudy skies will gleam blue.
I held on for dear life that's right, and it was the only life I knew.

Being sucker punched by your verbal denunciation.
Enduring the hurt because you felt like dirt.
Evoking self-deprecation upon me, but I see that it was you,
Who could not cope, so me being sucker punched was the only life I knew.

Indifference to the norms of divinity.
Therefore, stepped upon by divinity's norms.
Serenity for me, sincerity was not true.
However, I fathomed it somehow because it was the only life I knew.

Today I live. Today I love.
Today I cry. Today I die. I think so.
I must be. I have to be. That cannot be.
When this here…this is the only life I know.

Kiss of Death

Our lips met,
Our tongues greeted one another with passion.
We embraced, forgetting about the world
As we gave ourselves to one another,
In the intensity of a kiss.

Kiss....
Kiss....
Kiss....

Taunting the insides of my body.
Kissing making me bare.
Take away your kisses don't you dare.
But take away my soul somewhere to be relieved.

We are strangers now.
Wondering when our long departed friends
Will return to one another, or if so.
Softness-deceased.
Passion-released,
Kissing the grim reaper in its effect.

Kiss...
Kiss...
Kiss...

Once again we meet.
To heaven we retreat.
Creating sensational heat.
Our bodies now complete.

Kiss...
Kiss...
Kiss...

A moment of ecstasy,
Pleasurably next to me.
Kissing me passionately.
Causing the death of me.

<u>Happiness isn't here</u>

*Something has to be missing.
Who is there to blame?
What is the cause of this bitter atmosphere?
Why did joy bring with it pain?*

*Is this house full of curses?
Has my pride caused me to stay?
If the pain is too unbarring,
Than why won't I turn and walk away?*

*I know that the truth hurts sometimes.
But now it is very clear.
That what is missing is my joy.
My happiness isn't here.*

Nowhere to Hide

Safety-
The issue we have, but nowhere to go.
Without fearing the mad, malicious individuals that wish to harm us so.
Medal detectors in hospitals, security cameras in our schools.
Photo Id's in professional buildings, private housing we cannot choose.

The police fore no force at all when they force that force behind brick walls.
In times we need, they slowly proceed, contemplating a response to emergency calls.
Walking amongst the streets, with all eyes examining the air.
Afraid to look into another's eyes. No one wants to receive crooked stares.
Streetlights too dim, and no protection in a car.
Where can we go, I don't know, when nowhere seems too far.

Little kids petting animals, in a second they are shot just as animals.
Cruel beasts wanting to feast off others' dismay.
Afraid to leave the house day after day.
Wounded victims lying on surgical beds, revoking five bullets shot in their heads.
But that wasn't enough, the fight is not threw.
When he comes once more, once again trying to kill you.

Safety-
That is the issue, and now a roof cannot protect our heads.
When windows shatter and blood splatters
While innocent victims lie asleep in their beds.
Bombs underground, missing bodies can't be found
"America the land of liberty."
Well I can't walk out of my door, travel to the store, so liberty is not actually free.
Brothers and sisters step aside, put away our spite, our hatred, and our pride.
Understand all that it is worth be free,
Walking the streets without fear of our own city.

Forever Young

Seventeen years of comings and goings.
Fourteen years of memories stored.
On the burner there lies anxious moments.
And goals and dreams I can run towards.

Forever young always in my eyes.
Hoping to fight the demon's despise.
And when I depart, my soul will rest.
Knowing I lived my life at best.

Starting from the bottom, working my way through.
Searching for a way to calm the rough seas.
A smile of accomplishment, when the skies gleam blue.
And the journeys take hold of what I believe.

Forever young always in my heart.
Laughing and crying as friends come and part.
And when my maker asks of my life, and what I've done.
I will have lived several years with my innocence forever young.

Senses of Imperfection

*As I fall unto my knees asking God
To please forgive me for that which I cannot perceive.
I hear a crack of a chain,
Knowing that I am the only one to blame,
For keeping my emotions sustained,
In situations that remain constantly the same.
So I have not right to complain.
About the things I have not changed.*

*The halls reek as my subjective secrets leak.
Which keeps me cleaning for weeks,
Therefore I am never complete.
And the words that I speak to my beliefs,
Produce mockeries of me.*

*I taste the saltiness of my cry and my face is so dry.
That I cannot correctly identify,
I who should sparkle in my eyes.
So I've allowed years to go bye, not having realized.
That no matter how hard I try.
My deadly past I can't revive.*

*I am trying to touch the elusive, and again I am denied.
Yet numerous times I have tried.
To place the elusive by my side,
So that I could feel complete inside,
Not knowing that in order to touch the sky.
I must begin happily with I.*

*Raising up off of my knees,
I thank God for directing me to see.
That instead of me trying to accept,
I would rather project, and not correct,
That which is not perfect within my flesh
When I dissect, or better yet
When all of the outside world I forget,
As I connect with myself and introspect.*

*I must now admit,
That with every inch and every sense.
I too have weakened in the wrong directions.
And with all of my senses I perceive not yours,
But my own imperfections.*

Time and Time Again

Someone captivates our emotions.
Giving into the sensations once more.
Forgetting the feelings of abandonment.
Walking into closed doors.
Opening our arms to embrace,
The next one's life in which we partake.
Failing to capitalize; never learning from our mistakes.
Becoming overwhelmed with excitement.
Believing we've gained a special friend.
But the overwhelming feeling grows to boredom.
Time and time again.

Love of my Life

In my mind I am mesmerized, visioning the day we connect on one accord.
With every word spoken on our behalves representing love's true reward.
The troubles of the past behind us, moving towards a euphoric state.
Learning with every mistake that we make betters way to co-relate.
Me being your man, sticking by your side when times get rough.
Riding and dying for you, representing you; providing you all of my love.
And when you and I make love I AM...so embodied by your touch.
Kisses and hugs, felling your love and I just cannot get enough.

In my mind I am set free,
Liberated from self-captivation.
Free from all the negative relations
That spurned because of our lack of communication.
So if you understand what I am saying,
Than you too must have peace.
Knowing that one-day, somehow someway,
You and I will always be.
Starting a family, just you and me,
Making our house a happy home.
And even if weren't together physically;
Best believe that you'll never be left alone.
Because you're the one I want in my life;
Therefore, I do not want anything less.
The search for true love has ceased,
Since you've proven to be the best.

In my mind I am anxiously waiting, anticipating love so true.
With you being the light of my darkness, nothing is brighter than you.
Providing me with all that I need, from happiness down to stability.
Satisfying my every desire, igniting my fire, the key to my ecstasy.
You got a hook in me, and it just seems to never let go.
Taking me on a fantasy ride with emotions that somehow I cannot control.
But I would a fool to perceive this all wrong, and you not be one of a kind,
So hopefully stupidity won't get the best of me, trickery of the mind.

Boiled Skin

No memories of the actual pain endured.
Only Remnants of replenished skin.
And all of these years it has been ignored,
Believed to have adapted to, it faded in.

Unconsciously existing on the surface of my body,
Although forgotten the pain it caused.
I am starring at a picture of a three-year-old me.
With this same body wrapped in gauze.

Looking in this picture of myself so young.
With feelings of discomfort written throughout my face.
It's hard to even believe that I am the same one
Here, years later this image replaced.

I can't even remember how it all occurred.
My own skin boiling, I can't remember.
I just have to rely on my mother's words,
Of the day my life changed forever…

The lives it so ferociously scared-
The hearts it turned while boiling unfold.
As years passed many eyes have glared,
Over and over the story is told.

Me climbing up the stove to observe.
Being too anxious to feel my skin so bare.
A horrible sight as all stomachs turned.
An experience I am now unaware.

Graphed blotches are all that I can see.
No disconsolate feelings stashed within.
Years pass unrecognized by me.
Still it remains my own boiled skin.

The Ex – Factor (Factor Me Gone)

You are the man of my dreams,
But the key to my soul
Is still in the past, and I can't seem to go.

I have a case of the Ex-factor,
And all that I can say…
Is that I'm sorry if I've lead you on,
I didn't intend for things go this way.
I wish that I could push replay,
Rewinding back to before the gig begun.
I upheld the image of the honest lover.
Because I thought you'd be the one.
To make me move on from the past,
Only because my last lover
Did not complete his task.
And I began to become lonely,
And the whether is getting cold,
And I just couldn't stand the reality,
That I did not have any one here to hold.
You being the nice gentleman that you are,
With qualities surpassing him by far,
Causing me to speak,
Words of interest on your behalf,
Yet my feelings never peaked.
Indeed you possess all that anyone could ever desire,
But the truth of the matter is that,
He seems to be the only one able to ignite my fire.
So I am choosing the road of all honesty,
Instead of being a liar.
I honestly wish that the qualities you posses,
He could somehow acquire.
So you see,
I cannot possibly began to love you
While I am still in love with him.
But I do want you as a friend.
So this charade must now cease.
Me physically sexing you,
While unconsciously desiring another man's piece.
Even though it has been a while since his piece I received.
I am sorry to say, but you could not in that same way,
Be the man to fulfill all of my needs.

~Continued Over

So you're saying,
That I am the man of your dreams,
But the key to your soul is in the past,
And you can't seem to let go.

Well you can factor me gone
Because I am tired of hearing
That my qualities are outstanding,
However just a little misplaced.
That you long for all of my qualities,
Just belonging to another man's face.
I refuse to believe that I am the man of your dreams.
Because realistically you have me,
Yet you don't want me so its seems.
I mean your fantasy is now a possible reality,
Now explain that, you honestly expect me to embrace that?
After investing my, time, money, and effort into you.
Boo, I think you have the game confused.
You see I am not a second prize,
Only for you to pick and chose,
I understand that he has the upper hand,
Because I was once in your shoes.
Looking back over some cat
That is grimy, slimy,
With trickery being his specialty.
And you really would want all of this over me?
Oh I see.
Just don't get it twisted when you say that he's the only one to ignite your flame.
Because if I remember correctly,
Wasn't he the same one that extinguished it back in the day?
I'm saying let's just keep this real.
I do indeed know how you feel.
But I am not gonna to continue being your friend,
So that you can put me in this same predicament yet once again.
Honestly I am better than that,
And I will not be the fool once more.
I know that what I have to offer is the best,
Way too much for you to explore.
You knew how you felt when it all started,
Yet you wanted me around instead.
So that I could keep his spot warm,
While lying in your bed.
But you know it's so sad that you can't conceive.
That, just like me you and him didn't last
Because you could not fulfill all of his needs.

Untouchable Love

Too many nights spent alone.
Too many tears cried in vain.
Three and a half years and counting...
Still, no signs of change.
No hope for progression,
But the recession of our love is killing me.
Creeping inside of my soul,
Taking control of the last drop of pride that I have.
A part of me wishes that I never met you.
Because maybe then,
  I wouldn't wish that you were right here
  Next to me this very moment.
Holding me, loving me,
Erasing any traces of uncertainty that I have.
And just maybe I wouldn't hurt this bad.
I mean honestly,
You have become like a fantasy to me,
Elusive to my hands,
Unconnected to my heart.
A thousand miles in the distance of dreams,
You and I are apart.
No where close to where it all began.
Too far for comfort, too short for belief.
You see I must be a fool to believe
  That you and I could ever be,
Seeing as how after all of these years
  You've never loved me.
And I have just been chasing a fantasy,
Running away from the reality.

Untouchable love....
It is like a joke.
Behind all of the smoke of practical illusions,
  Mass confusion.
Too many words with ambiguous meanings.
Too many possible outcomes,
Leading to the one outcome that I cannot accept.
Three and half years in counting,
With nothing left expect
Distant memories of the time
  I thought we were truly happy.
When I thought that
  I had finally found the right man for me...   **~Continued Over**

*Now I find myself trying desperately
 To piece my life back together
From the day that you crushed it to pieces
 With the fallacies of your love.
It's like I have witnessed a bad accident,
And we are the drivers encountered.
Watching bodies crumble,
Shattering everything they were built from,
(Just like love, starting from the outside working it's way into the insides,
Until there is nothing left).
Being a witness to such destruction,
 You have no choice but to stop,
Offering your help to the victims.
Trying to get them to the nearest response unit
 That can possibly save their souls.
And later you replay that moment over,
And over, and over again.
Trying to picture a possible scenario
That would've preventing it all.
Trying to play God,
And control the destinies of someone else.
You see that is type of effect
 That our memories have on me.
And there is no possible way
 Of hiding this harsh reality.
Too many nights spent alone.
Too many tears cried in vain.
Three and a half years and counting…
Still, no signs of change.*

Back at One

One is the magic number.
Everything starts at one,
To sometimes end back at one.
But I believe that in a perfect union,
The precise equation equals two.
One body, another one's soul.
Now two bodies intertwine,
Becoming one whole.

And one is the magic number.
Yet so many long for two.
Two – be complete.
Two – Guarantee.
Two – fall in love.
Four – eternity.
You see one plus one equals two.
And two plus love equals
Two people in love
Four eternity.

That is why one is the magic number.
However, no one wants to be by himself.
To be at none, even though we are all one,
Created by the divine one.
Created in the image of likeness.
Unlikely to be alone.
Four someone else was created,
Four one person to call his own.

And, one is the magic number.
Still the precise equation equals two.
So to get to two, you must have two.

One person's love is not enough.
One person's commitment is not enough.
One person's honesty is not enough.
One person's emotion is just not enough.
All because a perfect union requires two.
Two minus one and the relationship is threw.
Because true love entails,
Two sides parallel to one.
One side short,
And love's never begun.
So someone is left alone,
Brining them back to one.

<u>Father to Son</u>

*Hey there little one.
You know you are my only son.
So why do you feel neglected?
I try to give but you reject it.
Still I am here for you, you know.
Although times have proven this not so.
I guess I wasn't actually there.
But in my heart for you I truly cared.*

*I have placed a roof over your head.
Provided the food that you were fed.
Yet you possess for me this utterly contempt.
I have bared clothes upon your back.
And you know this to be a fact,
So I don't deserve this childish punishment.*

*You are acting out, selfish and ungrateful.
Finding any reason to become hateful.
And I expected so much more from you than this.
Get out of my house I do say.
Just leave this home and walk away,
Because my goals for you, you did not accomplish.*

Son to Father

Literally you have kicked me out
As if I ever had a doubt.
That my whole life I lived for you.
You where my master I was your slave.
Always trying to please you, and to myself so afraid.

You honestly believe that you are hurting me.
Because you are setting me free,
Not knowing that I am free
Now for my own autonomy.
That is why I smile as you rage,
And you despise what I've become at this age.

True you've provided me with external worth.
But it is inside that you stayed away never putting me first.
Not allowing myself to me.
Withholding my happiness intentionally.

Selfishness must be a genetic trait.
Seeing selfishness deriving only for your sake.
Holding over my head,
Things you should've naturally done as father.
Yet I must thank thee, for allowing me to see,
That absence does make the heart grow stronger.

Broken Chains

I can't even begin to explain my reasons for coming to this.
But the feeling of self-cleansing appears every time I reminisce.
So I've heard that you bring relief, to those that sacrifice themselves.
That is why I am here crying, praying for your help.
I've been living a spiraled road, and the path is headed down.
My actions, my soul attachments, the old me I haven't found.
I am letting humans get me down, making my life a total mess.
And the storm and winds are threatening strong, putting my will to the test.
I have heard that you bring deliverance that can dry up all the rain.
So I am curious that in your deliverance, will it mend my broken chains.
I have lusted the unattainable, seeking salvation from the hands of men.
Who killed my motivation, my ambition, my self-respect formed within.
Searching the crowds, browsing the webs, spending hours on a lookup.
For a cheap site, one night, quick fuck, two nut, soul-tearing hook up.
It's got me doing things, and seeing things in a way that isn't me.
I've become the one I use to despise the one that I would call a freak.
Making calls late at night, all I because I could not sleep.
Holding my pillow tight while I dream of another man lying between my sheets.
And now when I look around, what do I see?
Thousands of pieces splattered, of broken chains that had once completed me.
I've lived my life always believing that I had to be the one in control.
That I had to direct, protect, and correct all that I didn't know.
That we are free, yes given liberty, given every opportunity to fail.
So I've gotten myself in a complication, and my eyes are telling the tale.
This ongoing battle I am fighting, all within myself.
But I am too scared to gain my liberation, seeking proper help.
Yet I can ask for someone else to love me, to care for me through my pain.
Hoping their security will bring me out the misery, of my forever-cloudy days.
And I am too stubborn to give to you God, your deserved praise.
And ask from you a linkage, to mend my broken chains.
Words cannot explain my guilt, of the way that I've let myself go.
I've become a completely different person that my old eyes would never know.
And even in simple decisions I have opted the road that goes,
Along with most humans you know, "Anyway the wind blows."
So as time carries on, the distance between you and I continuously grows.
Therefore I am denied the joy of life, the strength that I was once composed.
So God please forgive me, as I ask to end this hurting pain.
And God please protect me, while you mend my broken chains.

Burn the Bitch Down

Inside these wall nobody knows,
The malicious behavior that has taken place.
I have no proof of evidence, any documents,
There are no bruises upon my face.

Promises where broken here.
The promises of the love that we once declared.
The house of horror is now destroyed.
Because of the life of us that we so foolishly dared.

You spooked me too often.
Your emotional abuse occurred too much in the past.
My revenge has arrived and its you that I see crying,
While I hold the last laugh.

The match has lit and fallen,
Just after the gasoline poured unto the ground.
The walls are crumbling as I smile,
Knowing that I burned the bitch down.

A Little Patience a lot of Progress

In times when tomorrow isn't quite fast enough.
Today seems as if it's the only way that things will work out.
The overwhelming feeling of it all being so rough.
How long will it be, too many years have changed that count.
Holding onto the fate of destiny.
Forsaking the pain that is caused from failure's torment.
Never understanding what it means to wait patiently.
I will and only will move upon times consent.
What I thought long ago would never come.
Has come and now I see.
In times I feel that out this life I have not won,
Never waiting patiently.

Will This Get Through to You

No more words to declare my love.
My declarations have been spoken in vain.
You seem unbothered that I long for you.
Causing my constant pain.

Just when I thought there was nothing.
There is something left that I can do.
I pray for my forgiveness as I wonder,
Will this get through to you?

Because I cannot go on this way.
Me making a fool of myself for love.
My actions will make the ground laugh.
Evoking pity from above.

I am ending this torment you watch.
Pain too excruciating to go through.
The bullets go off, my last breath I love you.
Will this get through to you?

My Mind is Playing Tricks on Me

Your friends have given me the tea.
Being just as shocked as I.
Because it seems too suspicious now that your free.
You are no longer by his side.
But I thought it wouldn't bother me
Because my heart for you was through.
And I would've never seen it coming,
That I would now be longing for you.
You see my mind is doing shows
Because your story is incomplete.
And this cycle of ours has become old,
And I wish that it would cease.
I wasn't good enough for you than,
Why so suddenly have things changed.
For us once to be nothing more than just friends,
This situation appears so strange.
Not too long ago I found myself begging,
Hoping that you would stay.
And that my feelings you were neglecting,
So I decided to walk away.

My body is calling too loud,
And I can't resist.
Just maybe if I wasn't too proud
I could be the man you wish.
But you see my mind hasn't forgotten,
The ways you put it to the test.
And for you to call me spoiled rotten,
You've never treated me any better than the rest.
So I am torn between two entities.
And I can't help but to question.
Why it is so hard for me to believe,
The warm welcomes of our reception.
As we declared a truce to our past,
Still I can't disguise the obvious reality.
That in that fucked up race I came in last,
But now I am the one tasting victory.
Baby my mind is playing tricks,
And I wish wasn't so.
A lingering love I long to grip,
A curious mind I can't control

The Best of Me

I keep mentioning the fact that I am giving you my all.
And continue wondering why I have never received the same.
But in your eyes you are giving me your all.
And I can't see that two entities never love the same.

All of this time I've thought about what I have put in.
The energy, the time, and all that I have.
While blaming you always, for not trying to be friends.
Over emphasizing minuet experiences, justifying selfishness only my behalf.

I've pushed you and pushed, until you were ready to leave.
And now I sit wondering why it is that you cannot stay.
In spite of me wanting to give you the best of me.
I ignored what you've given, wanting you to give in my same way.

Now I have finally realized that my expectations of you are too strong,
Now I understand that you loved me the only way you knew how.
So I can't blame you for your feelings of wanting to move on,
But blame myself if we never again reconcile.

Five Step Creep

Step one he lays down while the other lies on top.
Holding each other with soft gentle kisses non-stop.
Embracing in passion, warm tongues with a lick.
Ready to encounter a night they'd never forget.

Step two a little more intense than before.
Necking and pecking as their bodies touched more.
Chests rubbing each other with ease.
Experiencing a moment they'd never believe.

On and on, on to step three.
One kissed from head to toe the other perfectly.
Not missing a spot, every inch of his skin.
Rising towers are ready for races to begin.

Movement takes shape, as clothes fall to the floor.
And bare bodies embrace the ecstasy of step four.
Him lying on the bottom waiting to be topped.
Holding on for dear life while pleasure engulfed his spot.

Stares and heavy breathing filled the air.
As they moved so slowly expressing their cares.
On and on reaching that ultimate high.
Gave them the warning that they had entered step five.

Mommy Dearest

Mommy dearest, mommy dearest how are you today?
Talk as fast as you can understanding that here I cannot stay.
Mommy dearest, mommy dearest how have you been this week?
Tell me practically, the time that we again shall meet.

Mommy dearest, mommy dearest where have you been throughout my life.
I've lacked the love of a mother; we were separated out of spite.
Mommy dearest, mommy dearest how we act as long lost friends.
We say hi, we say goodbye failing to realize the truth is where it ends.

Mommy dearest, mommy dearest only if time allows.
Time has caused this division, the division of you and your so-called child.
Mommy dearest, mommy dearest the contrasting live we had to go.
How it feels to be motherless you should ask me, that indeed I know.

Mommy dearest, mommy dearest we have played the hands we were dealt.
My hand is tormenting, punching me hard beneath the belt.
Mommy dearest, mommy dearest we have done all that we could do.
Yet we cannot regain years, the YEARS, that I was taken away from you.

Mommy dearest, mommy dearest when will this cycle come to end?
Meeting two days only to walk away and began this waiting cycle again.
Mommy dearest, mommy dearest my emotions I can no longer contain.
Much resentment, much despise for I know you're not to blame.

Mommy dearest, mommy dearest how so much since then have I changed.
That little boy with innocent eyes, in my eyes I am not the same.
Mommy dearest, mommy dearest from where now do we start?
After all these of being motherless, I've grown accustomed to being apart.

All That I Have (Ode to my Father)

My life is a constant gamble.
Taking chances with nothing to spare.
My family seems not to notice.
So I guess I don't care.

You would think that I have everything.
Sacrificing the necessities of this life.
But those are only additives,
To what would be my paradise.

This gambling sensation makes me complete.
It's my one hope that drives my veins.
Driving cold blood within.
Cold to my family; blood in their pain.

I am chancing everything that I have.
All that amounts to nothing.
So why won't I put nothing to good use,
With hopes that it will eventually produce something.

Hope for the Future

Don't give up yet.
Hard times come in this game.
You must realize that it takes extreme effort.
For things to actually change.

It's not the end of the world.
We must fight for our aspirations.
We cannot expect to reach our endeavors,
With fear, and lack of determination.

Just a little insight that I wanted to share.
Keep the battle going you must;
Never get captured in another's despair.
Set your morals, your standards only for yourself.
We cannot live off of the standards set on our lives by anyone else.

Opening Closed Doors

Stepping towards a future, hoping that it will an easy step.
Pushed backed by the air vacuum of fate, reciting that "its not your turn yet."
Grabbing for the master key. The key that will open all doors.
There exists no key of such power. Disillusioned that the master key was yours.

New Beginnings for a second.
Minutes and years the story is told.
Hindered by the barricades of life.
Trying to open a door that will forever remain closed.

Starting a relationship of new. Putting all things in the past behind.
New Beginnings produce old endings, and old experiences never vanish the mind.
Thinking that it's all over, clear of all worries brought to an ending.
Cycles, and déjà vu encounters, tackling us back to trite beginnings.

Peaches and cream for right now.
Everything seems sweeter than ever before.
Tongues expressing that there is no sweetness just yet,
Your are just pretending to open closed doors.

It's too late to finally come around. Life in its entirety has moved on.
The melting affect once held will be forever on long gone.
No need to bombard when the lock is locked rock solid.
Too bad so sad you once had it, but somehow you forgot it.

Once a prized possession.
Now it's no longer yours.
You must realize that it is out of your hands.
Attempting to open closed doors.

What it is...

It produces many tears,
Emptiness is the outcome of its dismay.
It is here from dusk until dawn.
It will never go away.
It causes one's delight.
And is the same cause for another's heartbreak.
It is a burden to me.
It is all too much for me to take.
It is the cause of many's evil.
But is the cause of other's delight.
It awakes to be kissed in the morning.
It ignites passionate romance throughout the night.
It drives men ravaging mad.
It forces women overtly insane.
It is a package indeed.
Part of which causes pain.
It is the result of being lonely.
It is too elusive to occupy space.
It causes many to wear their hearts on their sleeves,
In some cases concealing bruises upon one's face.
Many misunderstand its content.
It is often taken for granted and abused.
It has no biases, no partial opinions.
It causes many the blues.
It can overwhelm one with glee.
Jealousy is an effect of its strength.
It often diminishes, but never fades.
It can control one's happiness.
Most lives are initiated in its name.
It is the justification of lives once lived.
It is said to be blind and to have no remorse.
Have you guessed what IT is?

IT'S LOVE!!!!

Does anyone care?

Observing the plains-,
The shadows of those who have long departed before ourselves.
Encountering your theories, and your standoffish personas of life.
Does anyone care about those who have suffered abnormalities
At the hands of another's careless behavior?
The rain keeps falling; the skies are fading to the point of no return.
That little child's ego has just been scared for life.
His future character will be based upon these trivial aspects of his life.
Once more I ask myself, with a somber compassion. Does anyone care?
What about that girl whose inferiority of men commenced because of
Child molestation, or involuntary romance?
That mother of five whose life is slowly ending because of a natural
Disease inflicted upon her by no means at all.
Take the dirt from my fingers.
Rest my body while I still can.
Cry the tears of agony, of pain.
All of my tears are cried in vain.
Inside of myself lingers a question of countless response.
Does anyone care?
Awakened to villainous attitude of society.
The race that is run, to further endow ourselves over the next person.
Those who run the hardest are the ones whom lose themselves all for
Some prize of self worth.
Each stride over one's mishaps places you further and further upon
That sacred pedestal.
Because he is illiterate, since they are homosexual,
Because she is less fortunate,
Since society accepts my faults better than his.
I am now this monster of arrogance, laughing at those beneath my social status.
However my actions are justified because no one cares.
Empathy has invaded everyone into thinking as one,
And so many things are taking place, making it too evasive to care.
Justification is the key, controlling my destiny, my heartlessness
For this way too long journey.
Open polls for response.
Keep minds clear for explanations of the cause.
Still does anyone care about you, about me, about us,
About them, about our history?
I guess not, when we walk away from it too fast to even began
To think about caring.

Part II.

Spoken Silence

Open Mic

Here I go again man...
I'm just gonna try this again man...

You see I'ma try to find
A spot where real recognizes real.
A spot that don't have fake wannabee ass rappers
All up on the mic just to spit a deal.
Hating on the true lyricist,
The manipulators of poetic phrase.
True masters of the art of metaphors galore,
    With their prophetic wisdom being displayed.
Man I'm just to trying to find an open mic that's all...
Where I can spit some raw shit;
Where my sexuality won't be my downfall.
You see because I've been to many locations
 That advertised open mics,
Yet niggas wanna hate on me and shit
    Since I fucked a nigga last night.
I mean can I just be real for a second...
I just want to speak the truth....
Some of y'all wanna deny me the rights of my poetry
Just because I'm sexing dudes.
That's why I just need an open mic...
Where I can just say whatever the fuck I wanna say.
Where niggas aint tryna sensor me and shit you know,
    Just because I'm gay.
I mean honestly you don't have to accept me,
But I ask please do respect me...
Enough to not reject me...
And the lines of all my poetry.
I mean all I need is just an open mic...
Cause I hear all these muthafuckas
Talking shit about who got the tightest flow.
So what I say to that is duke spit your flow,
But youngin you better know
    That I'ma bring you the realest flow.
So, if you hard than you
Just might wanna bust that flow.
And if you gangsta than you
Just might wanna hit that flow.
I mean cause if you tight than you
 Just might wanna spit that flow.
And since I'm gay than just watch the way I switch this flow. **~Continued Over**

44

From fast to slow, brining ya'll the illest flow.
I spit that, kick that, mix that shit.
I write my words down flip em and reverse that shit.
Making some of these cats
Go back to their labs and rehearse their shit.
Saying to their selves,
Damn how this faggie come and verse that shit.
What the blood clot
Dis batty boi doing pon here.
Mi gwan bust mi guns;
For me no wan no punks in here.
He better run fast for mi bash his skull,
BUT DIS BATTY BOI
FI FOR ME BLOOD CLOT SOUL.

And still I'm searching for on open mic…
So that I can get up, and stand up,
Professing these words that I write.
Cause all I need is just an open mic,
So that I can recite the poetic reflections
Of my intellectual insight.
And truthfully I don't mean
To toot my own horn,
But aint nothing wrong
With being a little cocky.
Cause it damn sure ain't a thing you can do
That's really gonna stop me
Because either way you still find a way
To hate on the words that I speak.
But you best believe that I'll be
The topic of blasphemy in someone's poetry next week.
That's why I just need an open mic…
Since niggas wanna put my skillz to test.
So that I can keep it real for my peeps man,
Through these true words that I profess.

Fear Factor

Unjust mentalities causing harm to individual creations.
Where motivations and inspirations are spurned by the lust of mere infatuations.
Failing to capitalize on the blessings of prosperous relations.
Because you fail to realize that self actualization
Does not recognize materialistic proclamations.
Caught up in the moment of superficial lies, and meaningless temptations.
Worshiping God's that are intangible, and are idols of countless admiration's.
Twisted explanations of even more twisted and complex situations.
Initiated by a twisted image of one's self, their non-visible perpetration's.
Too eager to acquire in life endeavors that falls away from the norm.
Living an illusion, portraying an image,
Following the standards that society has formed.
Unable to recognize your true self, all of these years you have performed.
Repression, aggression, non-accepting, deception, qualities- keeping your torn.
With introspection comes an understanding, of inward emotions that inform.
When the clairvoyant lies prevents and disguise
The truth from actually being learned.
There will be no one else around helping
When you finally realize and your world begins to turn.
But around you now there are many waiting to
Ignite the flame that you eventually be burned.
Looking around wondering why new experiences produce old endings.
Not comprehending that in order to build a secure future
One must start from the initial beginning.
Too apprehensive to gain self-liberation,
Being a political campaign you are pretending.
With the surface solutions,
And commercial institutions that you are constantly defending.
Giving in relations' one third of your self, therefore true love you are preventing.
Yet you search for reciprocity, ignorantly masking it from your own recognition.
And I am not at all perfect or overtly omniscient in old aged wisdom.
But I come to aid the mistaken, by acknowledging the reality in false pretensions.

Breathing in Silence

Inhaling air. The air that has inhaled me.
Exhaling its remnants, those remnants living profoundly.
My breath is invisible; it must be when no one sees.
No one observes my existence, me being the incurable disease.

I wonder am I really alive. I am physically but mentally no.
I can't be alive until the eyes of society tell me so.
I breathe harder, breathing louder to state my presence.
I could breathe all the air on earth; still I breathe in silence.

Married with Children

To some of my females out there, whose husbands aren't true.
You think the mistress is Jane, boo only if you knew.
That your man gets down, and by that I mean that he,
Doesn't have another female around, and yes he is trying to holla at me.

He said that he was married with children, and that he is in love with you.
Yet there is something lacking underneath the sheets,
Something in the bed that you cannot do...
He claims that he is the prodigal father, and his kids to him are his world.
Yet he messes around on you their mother, there isn't another girl...

So darling I am coming at you with respect. I just wanted to you know the tea.
Your man came at me with sugary eyes because he thought I'd be his freak.
I dug deep to find your number, playing the game until I did.
Because it made me mad finding the wallet, picturing your beautiful kids.

All these years you thought that he was honest.
And that homeboys on the corner were just his friends.
And those nights he was supposedly watching the game,
He was actually tapping those skins.

While you were at the store buying extra butter,
And paying for loafs of bread.
He was lounging on your sofa chillin,
With lil youngin giving him head.

Boo I am sorry that I had to be so graphic,
Believe me I am not trying to make you mad.
But his actions have left me in total disappointment,
I see he wasn't the man you thought you had.
I didn't want to disrespect you, performing the acts he was requesting of me.
He gave me excuses of why he wanted me on my back
Because of what you lacked beneath the sheets.

So ladies I am doing the right thing right? But I am just the barrier of bad news.
And to the other DL brothers out here trippin don't think this couldn't happen to you.
They claim that they hate us fags, and to fuck around with us they wouldn't.
So why are so many of them asking from us ass,
Even though they are happily married with children?

Once Again

It seems here lately,
That you have fallen for me once again.
You exerted so much energy to try not to.
You exerted that energy only to pretend.
That to you I meant nothing, that my words did not effect you.
But I've heard the stories from your walls,
Of how in the night you fall
Singing how life without me is blue.

Its seems here lately,
That you have fallen for me once more.
Because your passionate stares, and your undressing glares
Tell the emotions that you try your best to ignore.
But what for,
Who knows why you wish to deny your own passion.
Telling me that you could care less,
But I know best behind the façade of your stubborn reactions.

It seems here lately,
That your mind is captivated by me this time.
It is you who wants me,
It is you that desires us to be together forever in time.
You can't admit it but I know
Because your sugary voice told me so.
Once more my love you take hold.
Once again you are the one in control.

It seems here lately,
That not a moment passes without me in your mind.
Your dreams so they seem,
Contain visions of you once more being mines…
As in the past which did not last
Only because we could not be friends.
No need for a show because believe me I do know
That you have fallen for me once again.

Kiss of a Rose

Pedals falling slowly,
Stems rubbing against your spine.
Symbols of passion arising.
Which one stem, yours or mines?

Rubbing pedals upon you.
Kissing the spots formed by the touch.
Having you here next to me,
Just alone means so much.

This moment will be cherished.
A love so sweet as to be kissed.
The intensity of our bodies flow,
While your image without I miss.

Bottomless Pit

Could it be that I am falling...

Fading way into your oblivion.
Turning away, staying for days crawling,
Underneath the walls of games that are constantly going on.
Because it's something about your eyes, and it's something about your lips.
That hurts when they say goodbye, and melts me when you kiss.
I am falling into your world, so catch me holding on tight.
Pit less floors, and opened doors keeps me armed throughout this fight.
And the sound of your voice, I have no choice than to choose no other than you.
So call construction for a hoist, it will take one to keep me falling anytime for you.

Could it be that I am feening...

My body yearning, my heart burning, my insides screaming.
Making love, enduring your hugs, please don't tell me that I am dreaming.
Because it is the way that you touch, that gets to my bones so much,
And yes it's the way that you move, that builds a fire in me too intense to cool.
I am still falling into your depths. And I can't resist.
Wanting give you the best, forever yours I promise.
My breath is speaking the words; that I know can be heard.
When we meet and retreat and my secret spot you hit.
Yes I am falling every inch of me crawling, sunken away in your bottomless pit.

Hoping for the Best

Keeping my head held high,
When so many things weigh it down.
Wishing that he would be there,
As usual he is nowhere to be found.
Looking towards my future.
And so many things that I wish to endeavor.
Comprehending the wise words of the quote,
"Never say never."

In times of need of a friend,
So many to call on to lend a helping hand.
Me being the caring, affectionate individual,
They can't quite understand.
For so long now I put it out there,
Giving away my heart with a key.
Not realizing that no one else can love me,
The way that I love me.

Praying that someone will discover my words,
Opening the doors for me.
Sharing my voice with the world,
In between the lines of my poetry.
Wanting to make wise decisions,
Ones that will allow me to reap my harvest.
So I must plant seeds in the winter,
If I wish to partake in spring flowers.

So from here on out,
I'll be putting my mind to the test.
The results aren't clear this moment,
Still I am hoping for the best.

The Limelight is Glowing Dim

Public eyes are watching with caution,
As masculine figures take a stand on life.
Placing themselves upon a pedestal
To later deny their sacred personas,
Supposedly created by society.
Young men are growing up with faulty guidance,
No honorable man to follow behind.
No footsteps to help guide the way,
When footsteps guide in circles, diagonal lines,
Horizontal plains.
We have wise men preaching that the youth today must be saved.
That the younger generation has no regard-
On life, of values, of dignity;
The youth by day is becoming more worldly.

The limelight is shinning and no man has shown.
That he should be respected, since he cannot respect his own,
Family, his wife, and the responsibilities of his marriage.
So how can young men realize that they too must respect themselves?
Presidents are setting the stage to act in public affairs.
And holy matrimony is so holy that they love to share their phallic tools
In others with intentions of gallantry.
So the limelight glows dim, forcing all men to withhold from being
Accountable for their responsibilities.
How can we see those in the limelight and try to make a change,
If they continue to veil secrets in the dark,
Creating a limelight glowing dim.

Home Sweet Home

After all of these year of love.
Where do you we go from here.
Do we part our separate ways to end it,
Or wait and hope that it reappears.
The children are growing older,
And our years are growing short.
No one knows just much how longer,
Our happiness can go without.
We've built a house from ground up,
Putting our life's work too good use.
But what use is a sweet house if we can't enjoy it,
Let us not mistake the truth.

We gaze at one another with contempt in our eyes.
Wishing we had done things differently in the past.
Frustrated that our vows we somehow forgot,
Which explains why they could not last.
We have memories of the love we once held,
And memories of the process of how it left.
Because of our selfish needs we could not proceed.
When it got put to test.
So here we are now at a crossroad,
Discussing over the phone.
The decisions that we must compromise,
Splitting our once happy home.

The Vibe

Chillen in the corner with drink in my hand.
Waiting for my song, that one special jam.
And as the DJ turned tracks, the party was lame.
Cause every since 9-6, shit just ain't been the same.
I was headed to move, as you walked to the floor.
Leaving me startled surprised, unlike never before.
Catching a vibe, thinking this must be the night.
Not turning my head moving my eyes, keeping you in close sight.
Thinking to myself, "damn how bad I wanted to holla.
I am losing my mind, cause man I am feeling this brotha."
I was hoping that he was there alone by himself.
The attraction in my eyes, my infatuate stares I couldn't help.
Just as I attempted to approach, someone else began to cruise.
Caught in my feelings, Because I was really feeling this dude.
I was stuck with a vibe, so I decided to leave.
But your stares caught my eye, seeing you too vibed me.
The night was getting late, and as I looked to my watch.
I heard the beat drop and I stopped cause it was cueing in Fox.
That's my girl so I swerved, dancing to the floor.
Moving closer to you, I just had to be sure.
I started doing my thang because I was feeling her beats.
As I moved I remained cool while you started to creep.
I'm thinking "oh yeah" this youngin knows what's up.
His eyes, and his vibe, its me that he wants.
Because the vibe was strong, and homeboy was so fine.
And I had nothing to lose; to make homeboy mines.
He whispered in my ear, could he have this dance
So I moved so smooth, about to shake fast.
I asked first chance could he handle all of this,
As I popped non-stop, nare beat did I miss.
But he stepped in and started dancing. Damn could this be,
That the most stunning man in here is putting it all on me?
Colgate would've given millions, if they could've witnessed my smile.
Cause God only knows how much I am digging this vibe.
So I made the first move by the exchange of our numbers.
Cause it was something about dude, my curiosity it wondered.

The Vibe Part II.

That night in the club shit it was only the beginning.
Because what was sweet at the start didn't have a sugary ending.
After the numbers were exchanged I couldn't wait for the night to end.
I was anticipating several mornings that I would embrace my "new friend."
He was all that I wanted, believe me he was everyone's dream.
His words swift, his actions proper, this is why I still can't believe...
That our friendship flourished immensely, so quickly off the break.
One week his friend the next his lover, never once did we date.
Things were oh so peachy, WERE being the operative word.
Pampering me with all that I could imagine, hundreds of dollars he splurged.
But all this while I was getting to know his gallantry, while forgetting about his soul.
But that too I would eventually experience, and this is were the story unfolds...
We wanted to keep our relationship in perspective, "let's not move too fast."
"Let's get to know one another on a personal level, with hopes the we would last."
It seemed to be working because each day was one better than the past.
We were definitely vibing, even with the issues we masked.
Several months went bye and we finally shared that special night.
All positions where checked firmly, all movements n-sync, bodies kept tight.
It was worth the wait because the experience literally blew my mind.
And even to this day I must say, that he was absolutely one of a kind.
Months went pass once more, but things began to change.
It started to seem slightly different, unlike those initial days.
After almost a year, I began to question our own validity.
I knew that I was falling in love with him, but was he out of love with me.
Our conversations became much shorter, always ending on negative words.
The outings became more infrequent, no longer hundreds did he splurge.
So I attempted to communicate, by means of a ring.
However, before I could get my chance to propose he too surprised me.
His words still so swift, but this time they cut unlike you could ever conceive.
He said that for a while he has been cheating, and in the process contracted HIV.
And that I too should get tested because I could be at risk.
Because he was heartless being a gentleman, slinging what I thought was only my dick.
Never did he apologize, never offered to wipe the saddened tears that I cried.
Eventually I would only see him in the exact place we initially vibed.
Shaking his ass just the same, with that same provocative look in his eyes.
Searching to make his next move on some other, another lonely naive little guy.
And as the story ends, I want to tell all that I have turned out fine.
But there have been several victims whose stories haven't ended just as mines.
And that if I could help somebody, It will be well worth my time.
But in the meantime just remember that all it is, is just a vibe.

The God in Me

I've been told that when I see someone,
To hug, proclaiming that I see the good in you.
That God is love, and love is for everyone,
No matter the problem you're going through.
But as I look unto this mirror,
In this still reflection that I see.
I stand asking myself one question.
Can I see the God in me?
Because it is so easy to acknowledge the blessings,
In someone else's live that we observe.
Therefore asking from God those same blessings,
While our own blessings we have ignored.
Even as he is with me everyday,
My humanly instinct constantly seeks more.
A piece of paper, a costly material,
Lost in a secular world trying to explore.

Still after Jesus died upon the cross,
Sacrificing his flesh, all to save me.
Just because my mother has noticed,
Can I see the God in me?
If our actions speak louder than our words,
And if in this next hour we suddenly die.
Would God's purpose for our lives have been accomplhised,
Or would our heavenly kingdom be denied?
Because I am a Gift of God.
Yes my name states that I am divine.
But is my character filled with divinity,
Or am I an empty gift inside?
If God is love, and love is for everyone.
Than where's my love if I cannot speak,
Encouraging words on another's behalf,
Displaying the God in me.

When I sing thanks to the lord for his greatness.
While I am giving my weekly devotions.
Do we really understand what we are thankful for?
Or are we just going through the emotions.
Because If we are all lonely souls searching,
For a quick fix or possessions that will make us happy.
How can I see the God in you,
If I don't see the God living inside me.

Winter Storms of a Nightmare

Windows crashing that is my life.
The way that I perceive things for me to be.
Winter storms blowing through destroying,
Frightening the life inside of me.

I awaken and exhale,
Realizing that it was only a dream.
But I fall asleep, falling asunder,
And now my nightmare has been redeemed.

It's cold and biting.
Freezing objects without a doubt.
Is this my home, my fortress,
Is this what life is all about?

Pretending that I was fully clothed,
Coldness covered somehow possibly.
Winter storms penetrating, and gaping
The wholes of long journeys and emotionality.

I see I've fallen asleep again.
Awakening in a pool of sweat.
There must be a monster lurking near,
I must have done something than I now regret.

Is this the end oh I think not,
When here comes more.
An entrapment a house of mirrors it must be,
With one door leading to the next arctic door.

Blizzard though it may be,
The snow is dark as night.
Black snow falling soaking away the candles
That Burn to produce my light

Ice packing-"the family"
Black snow falling-"the friends"
Wind howling-"my love"
All of which too implacable to make a mends.

~Continued Over

My nights are cold and alone.
Storms please let me rest, leave me be!
I dream of songs of freedom.
I dream of an end to this insanity.
The windows are still crashing;
Glass cutting my body grotesquely.
I know this feeling somehow adapted.
Glass stabbing my skin bleeding misery.

I am too terrified to sleep.
There is no one here to comfort my body of its scares.
When I fall asleep I fall in defeat,
Of the battle of nightmares.

And people stare but can't visualize
The winter storms on a summer's day.
There are the icicles, and polar bears of December,
When in reality it's May.

My coldness-"the world"
The bitterness-"my love"
My warming fire-"the hell"
All too implacable because...

More than a Man

We met on the simplest of terms.
I wasn't expecting anything, but was curious to see.
What the future would contain, killed by curiosity.
You brought to me an experience that I never knew existed.
You brought out a side inside me that no one had ever before revealed.
And as I embraced our new friendship with composed reactions,
My true feelings for you my anxiety could not conceal.
Still, here we are today divided by the exact reasons we began.
Unconnected, my notions rejected for you and I to co-exist more than friends.
Yet it remains to be seen that you have stood your ground.
Ceasing all communications, the possibilities of relations.
Because of my commanding love for you, you thought that I was obsessed.
Yet my intellect tells me directly from your dialect,
That you mean well in all sincerity,
But in all honesty I don't think that you're quite ready for me, yet…
You were the first to recognize my beauty.
Not only my physical, but my mental as well.
You were the first to recognize my pretty smile.
And I began to realize how much you were compelled by my smile.
So from then on I tried to smile at every opportunity that I was allowed.
Even when my insides were screaming, I pretended to you and myself,
Trying to control your emotions because of my longings.
During a time period where I was in search for a companion,
You road in on your white horse quickly sweeping me off my feet.
I was mystified by your interest in me.
I was dignified by your compassion for me.
I was justified by your expectance of me.
Could this really be happening?
Could I have found someone to possibly love and nurture me?
I questioned your warm receptions,
With every time you verbally speaking its validity.
None the less, actions speak louder than words,
And insecurities saturate any possibility of true love.
Years later I have grown, still true love I have shown
You, but you say that I am not the same man.
Baby; please explain because I just can't quite understand.
I've bettered myself in every possible way.
And my heart for you has not changed to this day.
Me constantly trying to love you with you pushing me away.
And you say…

*~**Continued Over***

Because of my commanding love for you, you thought that I was obsessed.
Yet, my intellect tells me directly from your dialect
That you mean well in all sincerity,
But in all honesty I don't think that you're quite ready for me, yet.
Limited of the fish to choose from the sea.
You caught my eye, my heart, my soul.
Capturing all that I was composed.
My emotions exposed, my body imposed
By your girth, and than your personal cream
Planting a seed, no your seed inside my walls.
And as the harvest bloomed, I assumed that
The fruit that I bared, you would reap, your appetite complete.
Believing that at your worst you would not seek,
Nutrients from another man's piece.
But you know what they say:
"That when you assume, you make an ass of yourself."
Still I assumed that you wouldn't take ass thrown to you from anyone else.
That what I had to offer you was best.
That you were intelligent enough to except from others nothing less.
Spending numerous nights sleeping by the phone,
Trying to breathe human life into its dead tone.
Confused as to why you weren't on the receiving end.
But the reality was that you had just recently met a new friend.
Leaving me alone, to cope on my own.
Turning my once bliss into unhappiness.
Giving to someone else the love of yours that I earned.
Them being the recipient of the prince charming that I yearned.
It caused me to lose myself, losing all my self-worth.
You were captured in the rapture with another man, for you I thirst.
Yes I tried. Yes many times I cried.
Yes to your demands I obliged.
Hoping that you would step aside,
Putting away your pride, walking by my side
And for love to me provide.
Nevertheless, now I am here and you are somewhere
That I don't know because it was beyond my control.
You see you were the first to let go; still I wish it wasn't so.
But that's fantasy, and in this reality I must move on, be strong, press on.
And you say...
Because of my commanding love for you, you thought that I was obsessed.
Yet, my intellect tells me directly from your dialect
That you mean well in all sincerity,
But in all honesty I don't think that you're quite ready for me, yet.

Reaching for the Untouched

Playing a game right-
    If you knew that I wanted to embrace you,
    Would you run to my side, with open arms,
    And with heart warming compassion?
    I am lonely, waiting to hear your voice on the line.
    Could you really be mines, wishing that my love
    Would be enough to capture your satisfaction.

Do you hear me calling-
    My mind, boggling by your actions.
    My heart yearning for you to use your key.
    To open and obtain what I feel would be real.
    A genuine affection shared between you and me.

Am I reaching for the untouched-
    Reaching for your sympathy, your friendship,
    Your time, your mind, your hold, your physical mold.
    Wanting to give myself to you everywhere.
    Dreaming, feening, screaming,
    That your eyes gaze into mines, that your body would rest unto mines.
    Reaching out to you, with you never there.

Feeling You

I wanted to kiss your lips so intense.
To show you how indeed I felt.
Your turned away, not knowing that the ways I kiss
Would naturally make your body melt.

You were willing to give little to nothing.
Opening closed doors, while I wanted to give my all.
All of my time, all of my mind, all of me…
I am receiving intensity, not receiving you emotionally at all.

I am feeling your body physically.
I am experiencing your expressions visually.
I am dedicated to our future mentally.
But I am curious to know if I have you personally.

Yes the sensation is nice.
Too nice as a matter of fact.
Building a sense of pleasure.
For us never to take back.

So you see all of this.
You undoubtedly have me without a clue.
But I have this feeling, this awkward feeling,
That I do not have each and every part of you.

Jagged Little Pill

The unspoken truth still remains
And reality I have not faced
I am still dreaming of fairy tale endings,
While my love for thee I've yet replaced
Denial has become my most favored trait.
A Hopeless romantic, forcing a selfish cause.
Determined to win a one man's race,
Striving for a victory that has long ago been lost.
Jagged little pill, so hard to swallow
Jagged little pill filled lethal, yet so hallow.
What was good is gone, nothing left to swallow.
Jagged little pill filled lethal, yet so hallow.

The pretentious of self-healing,
Of life without thee, of liberty without freedom.
Allowing me to deceive myself of the truth
My ears chose not to hear him.
Telling me "that it's over,
And the sooner I except the better off I'll be."
I couldn't except because I didn't wish to stomach
That he had digested me.
Afraid to swallow a matter of fact.
Afraid to turn away filled with regrets.
Constantly looking back deeply into the past
Praying for a light that would illuminate its path.
Searching for a way to somehow
Retrieve those lovely days.
The days that you longed for me,
Those days my mind continuously replays.
Jagged little pill, oh so hard to swallow.
Jagged little pill filled lethal, yet so hallow.
What was good is gone, nothing left to swallow.
Jagged little pill filled lethal yet so hallow.

Dismissing the wise words of souls that know,
Those that have been here done that and have turned out fine.
Dismissing wise words because I fathomed an illusion.
That their situations must somehow bare different from mines.
And that eventually I'll prove to everyone, that it was worth all of my time.
Missing out on the soulful cure of serenity;
The opportunity to gain a peace of mind.
This Jagged little pill is so hard to swallow.
This Jagged little pill filled lethal, yet so hallow.
What was once good is now gone and there is nothing left to swallow.
This Jagged little pill filled lethal, but in reality so hallow.

64

The Writing is on the Walls

A thousand of poems wrote,
Yet you cannot note that I am still obscure.
My words fly like birds, and again I have spawned more.
The depth goes beyond the abyss,
And the simple features of me you all miss.
Because you look at the background.
At how the frame decorates each letter.
Searching for diction, and syntax that I could've implored better.
Audience of millions, reading with their children.
Saying that I couldn't have hope, have dreams.
Masking my screams of freedom.

Ten poems shared,
But the recipient scared to take in each phrase
Hearts cringe, and emotional bonds mend,
As all of you all's startled eyes gaze.
At me, listening to my poetry, but not retaining a word.
While I voice my life, my strife,
And you later empathize the unheard.
You compare your experiences to mines,
Expecting me to see their similarities.
You people please you are deceived,
Living through me vicariously.
I am an artist,
Who paints inexplicable figures with colors.
That comes in the form of dialect unlike no other.
One poem thrown into the air,
And on whim I pretend like you and do not care.
Complementing me on my poetry
Because to you the rhythm is so nice.
But the irony is inside that rhythm
I spoke of sexism caused by you yeah that's right.
I am taking a plight,
Jumping off the edge to commit.
Suicide of your superficial smiles.
Fathomed to prevent my disillusionment.
Heaven's sin, demon's kin, spirits that I exhale in words.
So you attack me personally,
With you complementing my all.
Proving to me that at glance
You only see the writing that is on the walls.

Smiles

Laughter in the room.
Toys banging against the floors and walls.
Children at play, just listen to the way,
They smile and sing only elated songs.

Worries in their heads of what?
Not a thing, but how to have fun.
You think that their youth is ending.
But their happiness has just begun.

Pets, and hobbies in a delight.
Games that create all types of imagery.
Just image what the world would be like,
Without each child's unique personality.

A parable to learn from youth.
They're the wise ones, with their wise smiles.
The wise guy trying to create divine purpose for no purpose,
While children live life to its fullest that's how.

Brotha Man

Bills to be paid,
Notices' stating that money is due.
Exertion for what you ask,
Are these possessions worth going through?
Flashing at the wrist bling-blinging
Laced in Gabanna from head to toe.
Fuck the credit statement stating,
Fuck my baby momma hating.
Both saying that I can't afford these clothes.
How the fuck do they know?

My impression means the world.
So, I can hustle to gain the world.
Sitting on twenty inch chromes,
With my neck so froze.
See this is the life that I chose.
To have and to hold.
Supporting my wife on assisted funds.
But I am still fly, still shining like a stunner.
And you wonder?
How I have fresh Jordan's on my feet
With my family struggling to eat,
Fuck reality, I need fantasy.
Icy gleam, and Gucci Jeans.
Shit that I can floss nicely.

Man I got needs,
Fuck having kids to feed.
Baby moma's constantly wining.
Notices constantly compiling.

But my rims stay shinning.
My wardrobe stays styling.
And I am constantly profiling,
Off of loaned out funds,
That I will never return.
Even though I've been warned.
That criminal actions will be performed.
But I will shine on.
Until this brotha is long gone...
Fuck taking care of my home.

Flight 707

Baby I have so many questions,
So therefore I shall speak.
Of my growing affection,
That matures for you by the week.
I am wondering are you ready?
Are you ready for me?
Ready to conquer the world together.
Traveling along the seven seas.
We have come along this far,
Flying away, and now I want to start.
True love until the end,
Until deaths do us part.
You are the only one that I want,
The sexy star that is in my eyes.
There is no need for me to front.
That is why I am revealing my disguise.

Baby, are you ready,
To experience something new?
Are you ready for us to be together?
Because I am ready to fly with you.
Call the airlines for the tickets,
Arriving on time for the flight.
Because when you land there will be kisses,
And warm romance throughout the night.
There are so many questions,
Yet I am only searching for one reply.
I am in the passenger seat waiting,
For you the pilot that is my guy.
Who is the most beautiful guy in the world,
And no other man can compare.
You have the intellect, the moves, the words,
And I want to take you there.

I want to take you to a special island,
Making love to you under the sun.
I believed that we had reached our ending,
But I see that our happiness has just begun.
When we fight I want to make up,
For my fantasy dreams of you to become reality.
So baby answer me this one question.
Will you fly the world with me?

Kodak Moment

Looking into your eyes as you moved with passionate force.
I was startled surprised in all that I was encountering
Remembering crooked spines and soft voices of course.
A misty atmosphere filled with intense breathing.

Snap shoots in my mind how we moved, how you stared.
From the floor to me standing and you behind.
I must admit at first that I was indeed scared.
But now that feeling never escapes my mind.

I could feel nothing except you, only you, and you only.
While you captured what I set out for only you to find.
Reminiscing with chills in times when I am lonely.
Wishing that you would give again, but even better this time.

Photo memories in my head, how you looked as you went inside.
How you braced yourself and I embraced my special friend.
It has been a while since we played, you seek and I won't hide,
As we create a Kodak moment from start to end.

The Road Less Traveled

So many prospects underestimating,
And presenting me with small packages.
Believing that I will receive them
With my up most satisfaction.

They are willing to slide their hands down my pants
Take me home for their private dance.
Yet in my eyes that cannot glance,
And promise forever they will stand,
By my side, so they hide, denying me chivalry.
Taking the easy way out, as if they ever had a doubt.
That they intended to share my world with me.

So you bring me close to you,
Only in your time of need.
Complementing me on my honesty
With hopes that I don't believe
In love, in sincerity please.
You pray that in time my heart will heal.
From the way you tried to kill
Its soul when you fathomed it unreal.

You see they are willing to taste the sweetness of my back.
Just to keep me on my back,
While they open doors to relax,
Still my words they have forgot.

And it's the same scenarios,
Played out on different days.
The road bears right,
Yet they turn the wrong way.
Afraid to drive down the road into my world,
And the think that they deserve.
My pretty smile, my ultimate high,
And to be inside my inner cores.

I cannot believe they try to deceive.
Hoping that I won't plead.
For their soul, and my soul
The are quick to forever let go.

70

The Best of Me Part II (A Year Later)

It's funny how manipulations change situations.
Having me to believe that by acting normal I wasn't haven't enough patience
It is true that two entities can never love at equal amounts.
But it is wrong to carry on, when one's love never amounts.

I was under false beliefs that it was me whom had to change.
Into an image of old faithful, and for you to sustain,
The best of you, while even some portion would've been nice.
To be there for me to hold me as I cried those lonely nights.

Reverse psychology had me trippin, forcing me to miss out.
On true love, of the true happiness that I didn't want you to miss out.
Allowed me to lower my standards because you failed the test.
I thought I could be your teacher coaching you to be your best.

All while I fell, and fell quickly away from the truth.
That the best of me, could not possibly lie within you.
Sill I can honestly say, that my heart for you was true.
Yet that doesn't validate all of the bull's shit you carried me through.

Yes it has been established that I put in far too much.
But I can walk away with the honors of knowing that I can love.
And the one who needs love, ME, I will gain from above.

The journey will be long, but I will find a way.
To feel complete with me and only for myself will I stray.
I was lost inside of the sauce, trying to marinate solid flesh.
And as I thought I gave you top of the line, I am giving me the best.

Not wasting countless hours and seconds of time that is all much too short.
Because the best of me is so emotional, but I'll be my own support

No one Cared (Does Anyone Care?)

Visualizing a subjective perception of man and human beings of life.
Too much to comprehend, apprehend maybe,
Too much because it was real life.
Nobody cared!
Because I asked, "Does anyone care?"
Battling sorrows so you see,
Can anyone care honestly?
Showing remorse so they proclaim.
But ask them about you, ask them my name.
Branded deep in content for what,
The words seeped in one ear out of the other.
Given a rank when consciously asked
Not to rank this above or below anyone else.
No one cared once again I voice.
That what I am, I am not by choice.
The dismay, ironies, informalities, despair
All observed and through the processes received cold stares.
That family of five now has to survive without a parent.
That little girl now views disgust upon herself. But no one cared.
"Does anyone care"? Hell no in their heads.
They replied monotone, choosing apathy instead.
Dreaming of fantasies shared through some other.
They did not care that five children tragically lost their only mother.
They were invaded by the terror of empathy all subsidized into one mind,
Of bewilderment, mystery, of shock.
Could he be, could they be, could we be
Anything less than everyone else's standard formalities.
My pedestal has cringed
And I have fallen into the wars to defend.
My creation, my manifest, my art.
I evoked imagery out of the minds of empty hearts.
Focussing our attention to a life that everyone
Announces that we must live as animals denouncing our own to
Run the race better than the next wolf-man.
You can laugh, cry and mourn, or sit and wonder what I mean.
Awaken to the villainous attitudes of the foreseen.
But my faults are justified, but "Does anyone care?"
I opened poll for response, and to their response no one cared.

Piecing it together Somehow

What if there was no such thing as time.
Would we know where our lives are supposed to be?
And just what if this image that I see in the mirror wasn't mines.
Would I know how the world inaccurately perceives me?

We are all tying win the prize.
Fighting harder over the next.
And as the fighting comes to cease,
We are only one step closer to our deaths.

"There is a little piece here, and just a speckle there.
If theories were non-existent, would any of us be aware...."

Because I've lived a thousand moons, and observed several stars.
Yet there is something beyond recognition, that in my eyes seems so far.
Flexing muscles like the Don, whose strength flows... forever it will.
And this fantasy life would be nice only if dreams were in actuality real.

But what if there where no such thing as love and romance.
Would we shrivel as prunes dying in the sun?
Would we consider liberation under the circumstance,
Better yet would we find ourselves, imploring our own bodies for fun?

"There is a drop there, and a portion over there stashed behind that tree.
In life I wish it were all puzzle, shaping it piece after piece."

All that we encounter, and all that I have said.
Won't mean a damn thing to others, once each of us is dead.
So why should I worry of what they think of me now?
I am playing the jig, a lifetime so big, yet I am piecing it together somehow.

So you asked

How does it feel?

Do you really wish to know?
When our bodies embraced,
So let me tell me so.
Catching me by surprise, me standing on my feet.
You opening the doors,
Allowing our friends to meet.
Can I handle it we will see? I don't think so just yet.
Let's try again, and again this time
You must keep it wet.
I am embodied by your love, and it feels so nice.
My breath pulsating,
Breathing in and out that's right.

You asked does it feel good?

Oh believe me you couldn't possibly know.
Just watch the rhythm of my body,
And let me tell you so.
Inside and out, all the way to the top.
Hold me tight, and I'll keep it tight.
Making you never want to stop.
Lets change the position, all while you stay inside.
You've done your job,
So now relax and enjoy now while I ride.

Us breathing n sync, with love filling the air.
Do you feel me passionately?
Is this ride taking you there?
Taking it all in down to the core,
Moving side to side back and forth.
Keeps me yearning each night,
Wishing that we could make love once more.

So you asked how does it feel?
The feeling was oh so right.
Once again could our friends,
Share that feeling throughout the night?

74

Spring Flowers Every Hour

Every hour that I think of your face.
Every second that I breathe in fresh air.
Every wish upon the stars that I place.
Reminds me of spring flowers, every time that you are here.

Every call that rings throughout my phone.
Every picture that shows in it love.
Every moment that I am not all alone.
I am fevered by your hugs.

Every song that is song from out of my mouth.
Every word that is written in pin by my hands.
Every story I tell what my life is all about.
Your flower blooms, while you understand.

Every minute that I have together with you.
Every experience that I partake in with you by the hour.
Every kiss I receive from the kiss that you blew.
Blooms inside me just as spring flowers.

The Bastard Child in Me

Heavenly father, am I worthy of thee?
Because their words have forbidden, and I am curious you see...

They state your divine purpose, they state your settled way.
They state that my soul will crumble, if I live this life being gay.

Because of my lifestyle. Yeah it's that.
They hit me with lies, stating their facts.

They deny me my father, and I've tried to plead.
But they won't allow my pardon if I don't change within me.

They set out to heal, to remove the shackles upon me feet.
Yet they kill me with their theories, so me in bondage they keep.

They define all behaviors, and give solutions to be free.
But they denounce on my queen-dom because in their eyes they do not see.

That my love is an entity, still not different from theirs.
So their tools are useless here, where nothing needs repair.

Why can't I love you, when everyone has his own life?
And what is the purpose of living mines, since they say it's not right?

Please father excuse me if I am distanced, believe me its not by choice.
You see they have censored your existence, from my homosexual voice.

They say it is the only way, but I do not understand how.
Because of me being gay, I'm viewed a fatherless child.

About "Nate Diggidy"

Born in November 1982 I have lived in the D.C. metropolitan area for all of my life.

Graduating from Friendly High School in Fort Washington, MD, I currently attend Strayer University in pursuit of a Bachelors Degree in Accounting. I aspire to become a CPA along with pursuing other interest and talents that I obtain.

As a young homosexual African American, I have been faced with many adversities throughout my life. As a child I was teased and tormented by my peers being called derogatory names such as faggot, and sissy. Not even understanding the premises behind such words, as a child I had to endure that torment; because my swagger had a rhythmical strut to it, my voice bared a unique accent, and I didn't like to participate in the typical activities that many young boys my age engaged in.

I began to find solace in myself, really getting to know why I was the way I was, building up an immunity to the negative receptions that was created around me. I began writing poetry at the age of thirteen as an assignment for an eighth grade English class. Soon after I took up writing poetry as a hobby, and as my fellow peers, teachers, and family members caught on to my talent I began to realize that I had found a unique way to express myself through words.

When I came to terms with my sexuality at the tender age of sixteen, I began to write about more controversial and universal topics in my poetry, which has become a permanent fixture in my writings. As I experienced my first love with another man my heart was opened to expressing my feelings and myself very deeply. As this relationship began to encounter many obstacles producing outcomes of depression, insecurity, and promiscuity on my behalf, I began to express my self-thoughts and the hurt that I was feeling through my poetry.

So here I am now on the verge of twenty-one years old, leaving behind my adolescent years; about to embrace the future of manhood, I have brought with me valuable life learned lessons through many of my experiences, and those immediately around me. My writings spectrum has broadened not only to contain poetry, but many short stories, and the beginning stages of a novel.

-Nathaniel

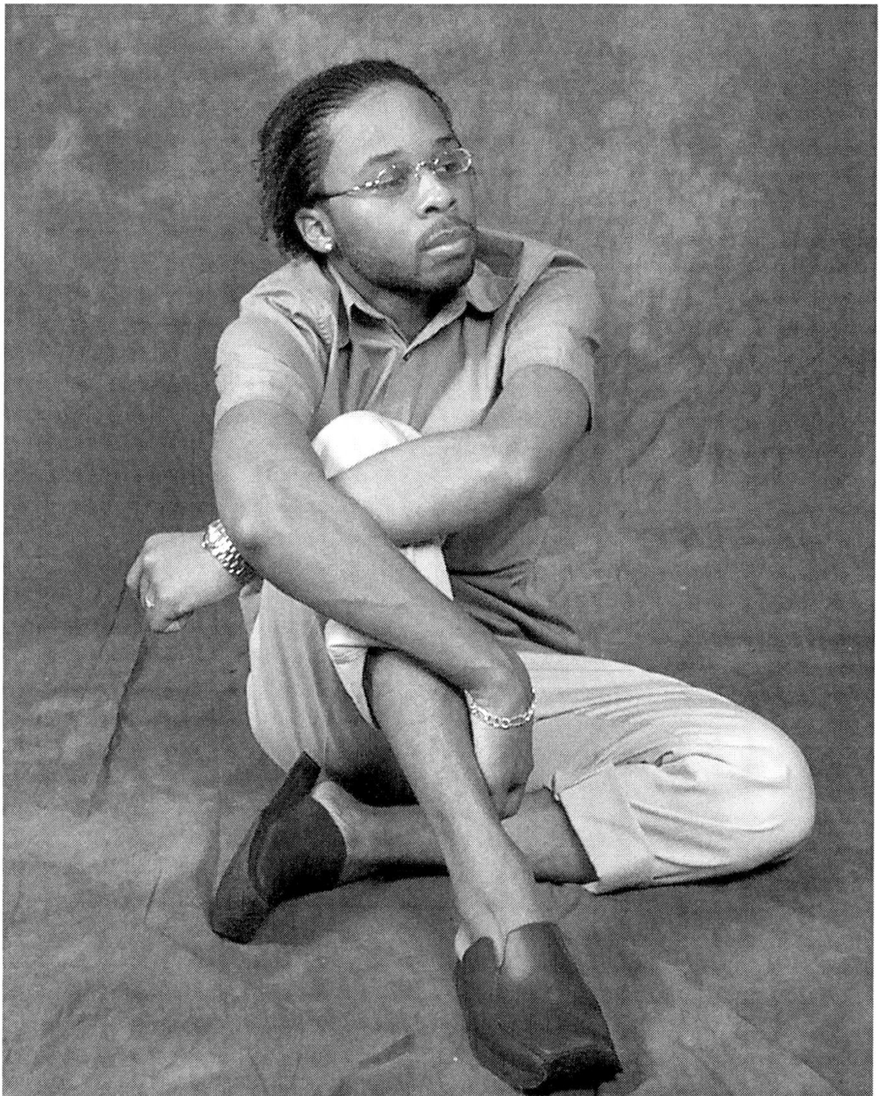